EMERGENCY RESCUE

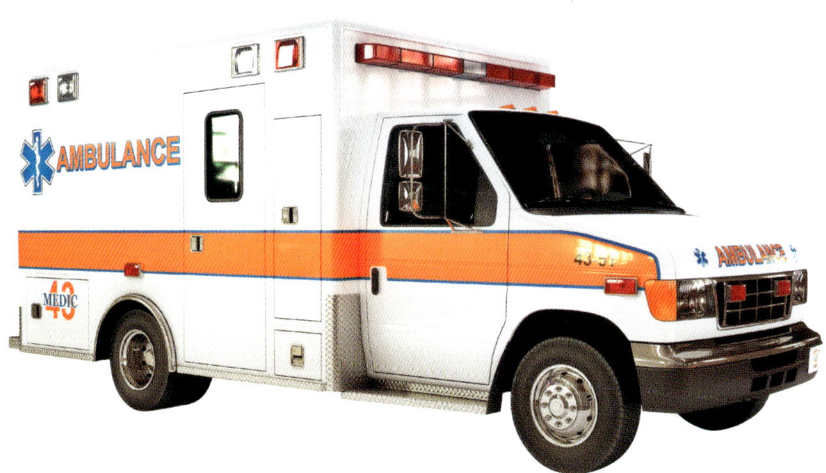

Produced for DK by WonderLab Group LLC
Jennifer Emmett, Erica Green, Kate Hale, *Founders*

Editor Maya Myers; **Photography Editor** Kelley Miller; **Managing Editor** Rachel Houghton; **Designers** Project Design Company; **Researcher** Michelle Harris; **Copy Editor** Lori Merritt; **Indexer** Connie Binder; **Proofreader** Susan K. Hom; **Series Reading Specialist** Dr. Jennifer Albro

First American Edition, 2026
Published in the United States by DK Publishing, a division of Penguin Random House LLC
1745 Broadway, 20th Floor, New York, NY 10019

26 27 28 29 30 10 9 8 7 6 5 4 3 2 1
001-345895-May/2026

Published in Great Britain by Dorling Kindersley Limited

HC ISBN: 978-0-5939-6649-5
PB ISBN: 978-0-5939-6648-8

DK books are available at special discounts when purchased in bulk for sales promotions, premiums, fund-raising, or educational use.
For details, contact:
DK Publishing Special Markets, 1745 Broadway, 20th Floor, New York, NY 10019
SpecialSales@dk.com

Printed and bound in China

Super Readers Lexile® levels 620L to 790L

The publisher would like to thank the following for their kind permission to reproduce their images:
a=above; c=center; b=below; l=left; r=right; t=top; b/g=background
123RF.com: Scott Betts 1; **Alamy Stock Photo:** Abaca Press / Nicolas Gouhier 42br, PA Images / Jane Barlow 19cra, PA Images / Lewis Whyld 45; **Dreamstime.com:** Bdingman 41br, Dmitry Bruskov 35cr, Candybox Images 36cl, Cateyeperspective 8tr, Mike Clegg 15b, Jiong Dai / Daedal 12bl, Elantsev 27br, Feverpitched 14br, Cindy Goff 23, Raisa Kanareva 11tl, Ivan Kokoulin 21cra, Nikkytok 26crb, Arisha Singh 15tr, Tlovely 14bl, Wave Break Media Ltd 19c; **Getty Images:** Cavan Images / Christopher Kimmel / Alpine Edge Photography 40, Moment / Douglas Sacha 16-17 (Background), Stocktrek Images 40cl; **Getty Images / iStock:** DigitalVision / Siri Stafford 12r, E+ / Bluecinema 9cla, E+ / Drazen 6, E+ / Kaisphoto 42-43 (Background), E+ / Kali9 15, 33tl, E+ / Leezsnow 34tl, E+ / LPETTET 18bl, 44t, E+ / MarkCoffeyPhoto 8br, E+ / Mayur Kakade 9crb, E+ / Pyrosky 24-25 (Background), E+ / South_Agency 33br, E+ / Sturti 7cra, EvgeniyShkolenko 44br, Joecho-16 12-13 (Background), Kali9 9tr, Valerie Loiseleux 22b, Cristian Martin 26-27, MichaelGMeyer 19tl, MJ_Prototype 30, peakSTOCK 31tr, Tashka 4-5, TheaDesign 8-9 (Background); **Reuters:** Kim Kyung-Hoon 43br; **Shutterstock.com:** Jaromir Chalabala 36b, Steve Hamann 11c, Derek Hatfield 17cr, Juiced Up Media 13tr, Ververidis Vasilis 23cr, Mahathir Mohd Yasin 10, Yiistocking 22cra

Cover images: *Front:* **Getty Images / iStock:** Chalabala; *Back:* **Dreamstime.com:** Ikonstudio cl, Poemsuk Kinchokawat cra

www.dk.com

This book was made with Forest Stewardship Council™ certified paper – one small step in DK's commitment to a sustainable future.
Learn more at www.dk.com/uk/information/sustainability

EMERGENCY RESCUE

Camilla Gersh

Contents

TRAFFIC

What's Your Emergency?

It's an emergency! Someone is in danger. They need urgent help. What should you do?

If you're in the US or Canada, call 911. This is the telephone number for emergency services. Your call will be answered by an emergency dispatcher. Emergency dispatchers are trained to handle lots of different situations. Their job is to tell police, fire, or medical services about emergencies.

Emergency Phone Numbers Around the World

112, 999	UK
100, 101, 102, 103	India
000, 112	Australia
107	South Africa

The dispatcher will ask you what the emergency is and where it is happening. A computer can usually detect your location. But the dispatcher will ask for your address anyway.

The dispatcher will note the details of your emergency. Then, they will contact your nearest police, fire department, or ambulance service. All this happens in just a few minutes.

The loud noise of a siren means emergency services are on their way. The siren tells other drivers to get out of the way!

What to Do in an Emergency

Call emergency services

Only call emergency services if someone or something is in immediate danger.

- Say your name and where you are.
- Explain why you need help.
- Stay on the phone.
- Follow the dispatcher's instructions.

If there's a fire

- Remember: try to stay calm.
- Leave the building as quickly as you can.
- If you can't get out of the building, go to a window so rescuers can see you.
- Crawl on the floor if there is smoke.
- Don't go back into the building.

If you need the police

- Try to find a safe place right away.

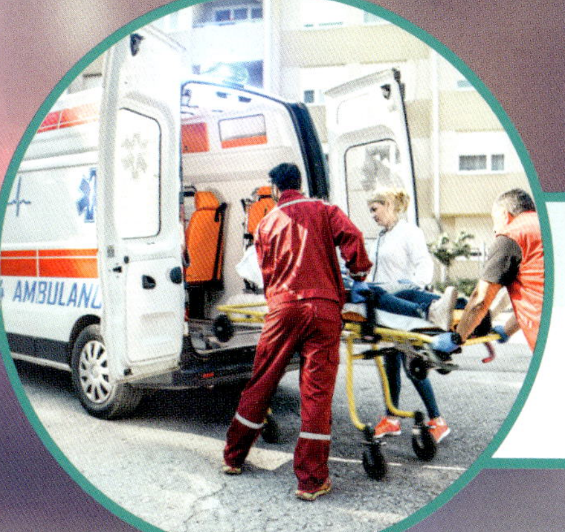

If you need a doctor

- Don't move a person who is sick or hurt.

Be prepared for an emergency

- Memorize your parents' or caregivers' phone numbers.
- Talk with your parents or caregivers about what to do in different emergencies.
- With the people you live with, pick a safe place to go in case of emergencies. This could be the house of a neighbor you trust.

Police

The police usually handle emergencies that involve crime. A crime is what happens when someone breaks the law.

Help! Somebody broke into our house. Please come!

Police respond to different emergencies. They help when there is an accident on the road. Specially trained police help in situations such as rescuing hostages.

If You See Something, Say Something

People can help police stop crimes by reporting suspicious activity. This might include seeing a stranger trying to open the windows of a neighbor's house. You should report suspicious activity by calling emergency services.

Many police officers patrol neighborhoods to keep them safe. Some police drive patrol cars. Others ride on bicycles or horses. Police sometimes use boats or helicopters.

A police officer has a badge that shows they are part of the police force. Police often wear uniforms. The uniform shows that they are police officers. Sometimes, police wear protective clothing as part of their uniform.

Many police officers wear small video cameras called body cams. These record what happens when officers answer a call. They can be used to show what really happened when officers were on the scene. Cameras and community partners can help make sure police treat all people fairly.

Police need special equipment to do their job. They have a radio so they can speak to other police. They use handcuffs so suspected criminals can't get away.

If you want to be a police officer, you need to be physically fit. Police cadets train at a police academy. There, they learn about the laws of the community they will be working in. They learn first aid, so they can help people who've been hurt. They learn how to use the equipment they will need for their jobs.

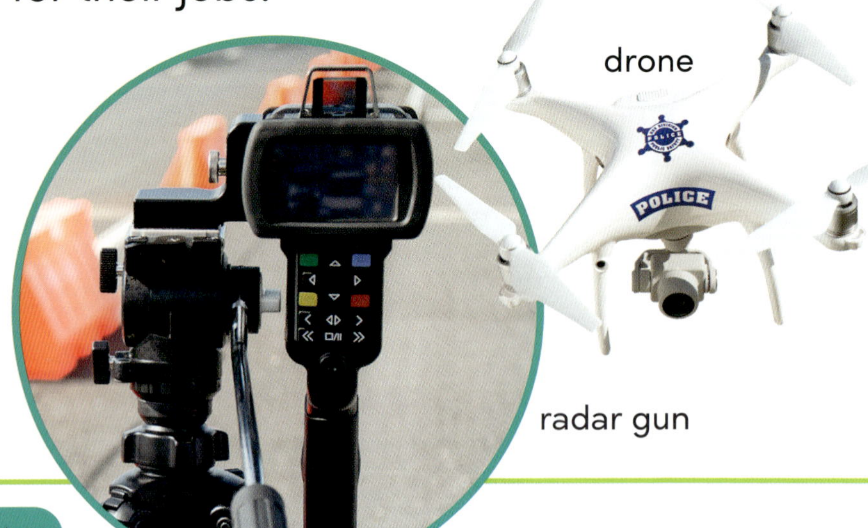

drone

radar gun

They also need to do field training. Officers in training team up with an experienced officer to get practice on the job. They learn what to do in different situations once they become police officers.

US Police Radio Codes

In some places, emergency dispatchers speak to the police on radios. They use special codes. Here are a few common codes for US police.

10-4	OK
211	Robbery
503	Stolen vehicle
901	Ambulance needed
904	Fire
999	Officer needs help. EMERGENCY!
Code 1	Normal. Take this call next.
Code 2	Urgent! Hurry, but follow traffic laws. No flashing lights or siren.
Code 3	Emergency! Use flashing lights and siren.
Code 4	No further assistance needed.

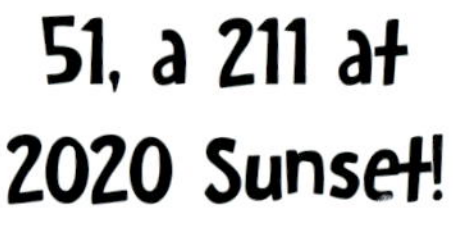

This means: "Calling police officer with badge number 51. There's a robbery at the address 2020 Sunset Street."

UK Police Radio Codes

In the UK, only a few codes are used. They tell the dispatcher what police officers are doing. Here are some of these status codes.

1	On duty
2	Available
6	On the scene
9	Arrest made

Fingerprints

Sometimes, criminals leave fingerprints behind. Everyone's fingerprints are unique, so they can be a useful clue in identifying a criminal.

1. Dust the surface with fine powder and a soft brush.
2. Press clear tape onto the dusted print, then peel it off.
3. Identify the fingerprints through searching a police database.

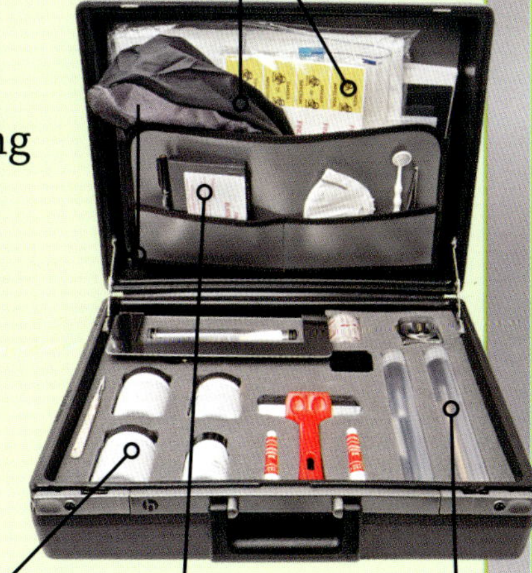

Fire

Firefighters put out fires. They also rescue people from fires and provide first aid. When they receive an emergency call, they zoom to the scene in a fire truck as quickly as they can.

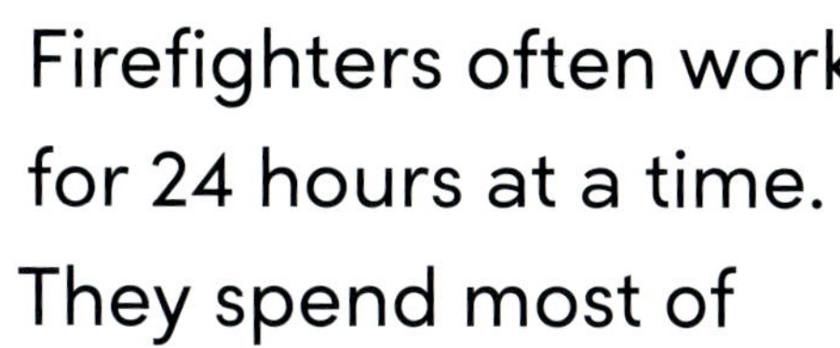

Firefighters often work for 24 hours at a time. They spend most of their days doing jobs around the fire station. They exercise, train, and practice drills for emergencies.

Firefighters on a training tower

Sometimes, they teach people how to prevent fires. They might even come to your school!

Fire trucks are loaded with equipment. They have ladders, fire extinguishers, and first-aid supplies. They have tools for breaking down doors and for cutting cars open.

Some fire trucks also carry about 1,000 feet (305 m) of fire hose. Firefighters pump water from the fire truck through the hose. They spray water on the fire to put it out. They can also hook the hose up to a fire hydrant if one is nearby.

Firefighters need to be strong and physically fit. They also have to stay calm under pressure.

Training for firefighters is hard work. Firefighters are tested for strength and endurance. They train by carrying heavy weights up and down ladders or stairs.

Firefighters learn about fire and how it can spread. They learn how to use firefighting equipment. They also learn about dangerous chemicals so they can make places safe after a chemical leak or spill. Firefighters practice rescuing people from car accidents, too. They learn first aid for burns, shock, and smoke inhalation. They learn CPR.

Firefighters often have to get very close to fires. Their clothing and equipment protect them. The gear they wear to a fire can weigh up to 75 pounds (34 kg).

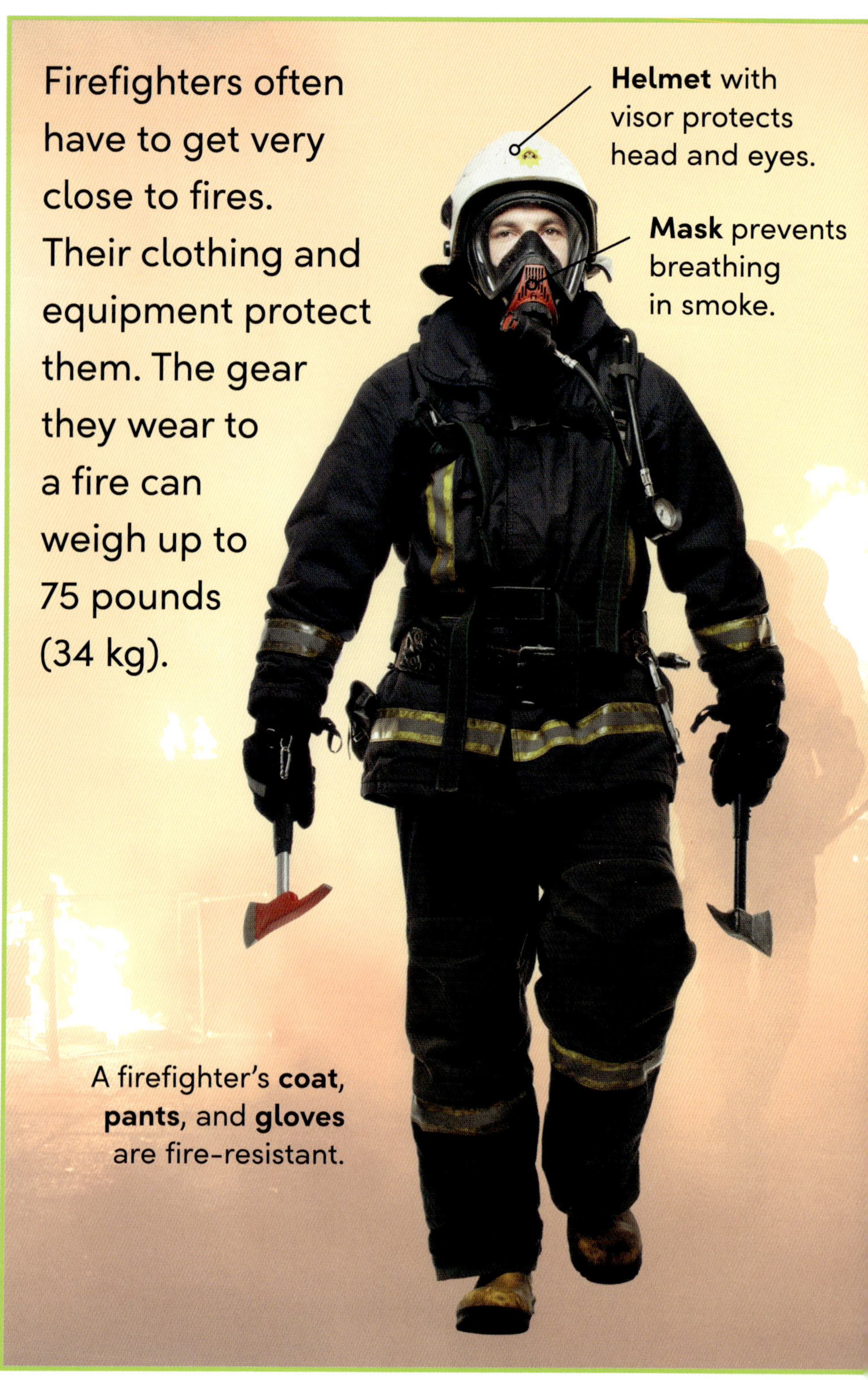

Tank is filled with fresh air.
Hood protects neck.
Boots with steel toes protect firefighters' feet.
Radio is used to speak to other firefighters.

Three things are needed for a fire: air, heat, and fuel. Paper, wood, and gasoline are some examples of fuel. To put out a fire, firefighters usually try to get rid of the air and heat by covering the fire with lots of water.

Fire Safety

Most fires happen by accident. Knowing what to do in case of fire can keep you safe.

- If you hear a smoke alarm, smell smoke, or see fire, get outside.
- Know two ways to get out of any room. Feel a door before you open it. If it is hot, go out the other way.
- Crawl low to keep from breathing in smoke.
- Don't go back inside for anything.
- Call emergency services.

In a forest fire, firefighters often try to remove the fuel, too. Trees are the fuel in a forest fire. If firefighters destroy the trees in the fire's path, there will be no more trees for the fire to burn. By destroying some trees, they can save the rest of the forest.

Ambulance

Emergency medical technicians, or EMTs, give emergency medical care. They are trained in first aid and other kinds of medical treatment. EMTs often drive to emergencies in ambulances, which have sirens just like police cars and fire trucks. EMTs help if someone has an accident, like a car crash. They also help if someone has a sudden, serious illness, such as a heart attack. EMTs provide quick medical care as soon as they arrive. Then, they take people to the hospital, where medical staff can give the patients further treatment.

EMTs carry lots of important equipment in the ambulance. The ambulance is stocked with bandages and other basic first-aid supplies. It has a stretcher to carry patients. EMTs have oxygen tanks, masks, and other equipment to help people breathe. They have equipment for measuring heart rates and blood pressure, too.

The ambulance has a defibrillator. This machine uses electricity to help make someone's heart start beating properly again.

EMTs wear gloves and masks when they're taking care of people. This prevents germs passing between EMTs and patients.

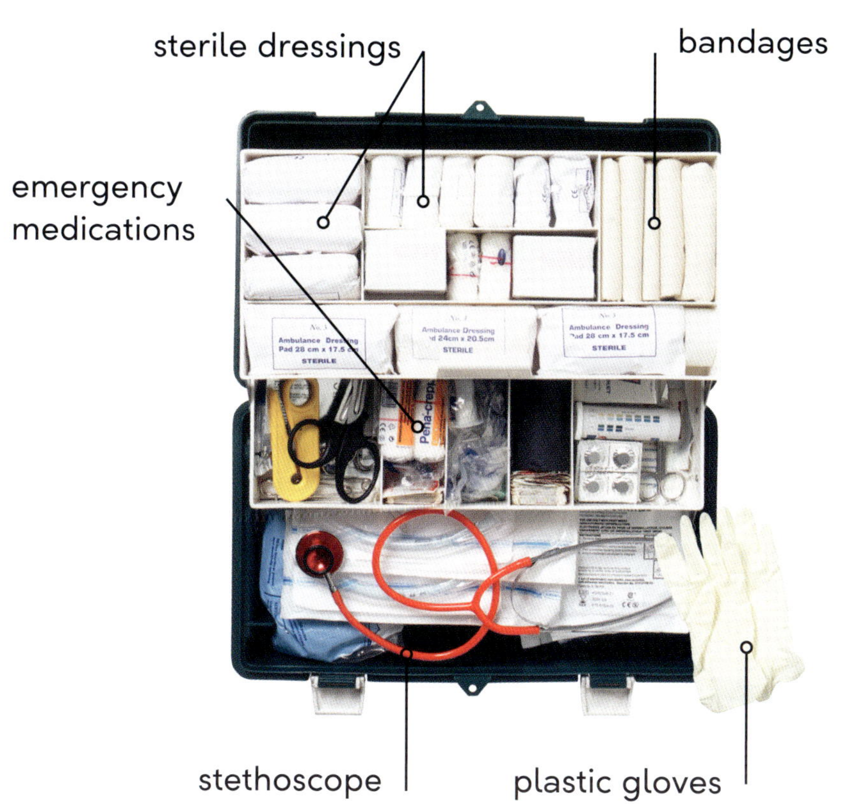

To be an EMT, you must be able to stay calm and make decisions quickly. You also need to be physically fit and strong enough to lift patients.

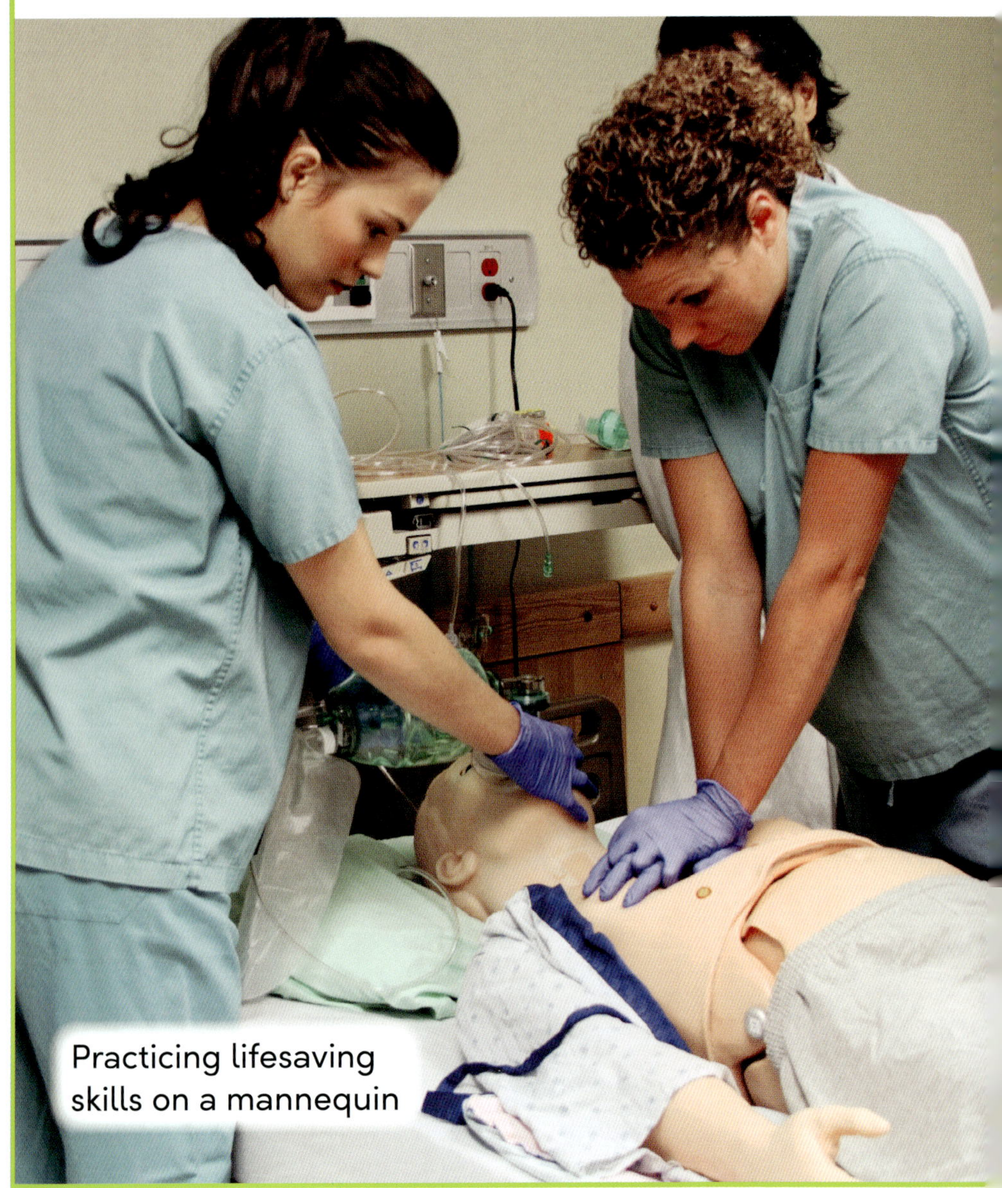

Practicing lifesaving skills on a mannequin

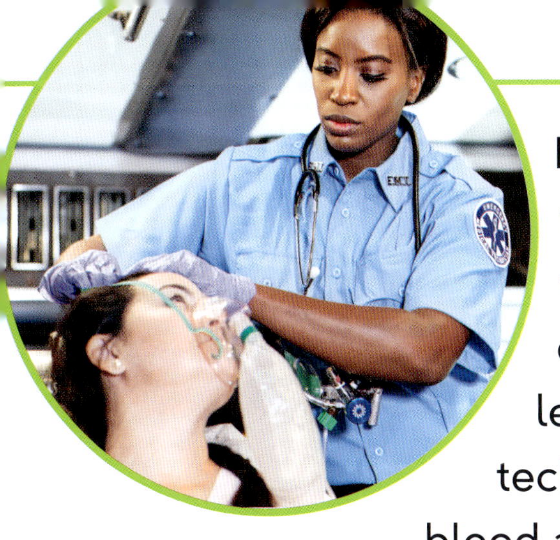

EMTs have special training to deal with medical emergencies. They learn lifesaving techniques to keep blood and oxygen circulating through the body. They learn to monitor a patient's vital signs, including breathing and pulse. They learn to put bandages on different types of wounds.

There are different levels of EMTs. Paramedics have the most training. They can provide advanced medical care. Other types of EMTs can provide first aid. They can give patients oxygen and some medication. Police officers and firefighters can also be trained as EMTs.

LONDON
AMBULANCE
SERVICE
7585

EMTs don't just travel in ambulances. They might arrive at an emergency in a helicopter or on a boat. EMTs even travel on bicycles and snowmobiles. All kinds of transportation are used to save people's lives.

Special Services

Help! I'm stuck on a mountain and I can't get back down!

Some emergency services are needed for specific situations. A search-and-rescue team finds lost people and rescues them from dangerous situations.

People may need to be rescued from places that are hard to reach. These places include oceans, forests, mountains, deserts, caves, or mines. The search-and-rescue team often uses helicopters to search from above. Once the rescue team locates the person who needs help, they may use other vehicles and equipment for the rescue.

Search-and-rescue teams are not normally needed every day, so some teams are made up of volunteers. This means they give up their time to help others even though they don't get paid. But like other emergency teams, rescuers usually have specialized training. They learn how to use special search-and-rescue equipment. They also learn first aid and survival skills.

Search-and-rescue teams are especially good at following tracks to find clues about people who are missing. Many are also good at other outdoor skills, such as boating or climbing mountains.

USAF

Emergency relief is a special service that brings food, water, and other urgent supplies to people affected by big emergencies. Disasters such as earthquakes, hurricanes, and blizzards can affect a lot of people across a wide area. Emergency relief teams may drop supplies from planes or helicopters if they can't reach affected areas.

Specially trained volunteers help provide emergency relief around the world. They work with police, firefighters, EMTs, and search-and-rescue teams to help people survive disasters and get their lives back to normal as quickly as possible.

Mules to the Rescue

In 2024, a hurricane destroyed many roads and bridges in the mountains of North Carolina. Teams of mules delivered food, medicine, and supplies to people who were stuck where no vehicles could go.

Rescue Animals

Animals are also used in emergency services.

Dogs

Dogs have an incredible sense of smell. They can be trained by the police to find illegal things like drugs and bombs. They're also very good at finding people. They can follow a trail with their noses, using the smell from a person's clothing.

Horses

Horses are used by both police and search-and-rescue teams. They can go places where cars can't drive. Horses might even be trained to find people using their sense of smell.

Rats

Scientists are training rats to search for people in places that humans can't reach. African giant pouched rats have learned to sniff out land mines and disease. They could learn to search through rubble to find survivors after an earthquake or bombing.

Cockroaches

Researchers have put tiny solar-powered backpacks on Madagascar hissing cockroaches that allow them to control the insect's movements. These cyborg roaches could help find people trapped in small spaces.

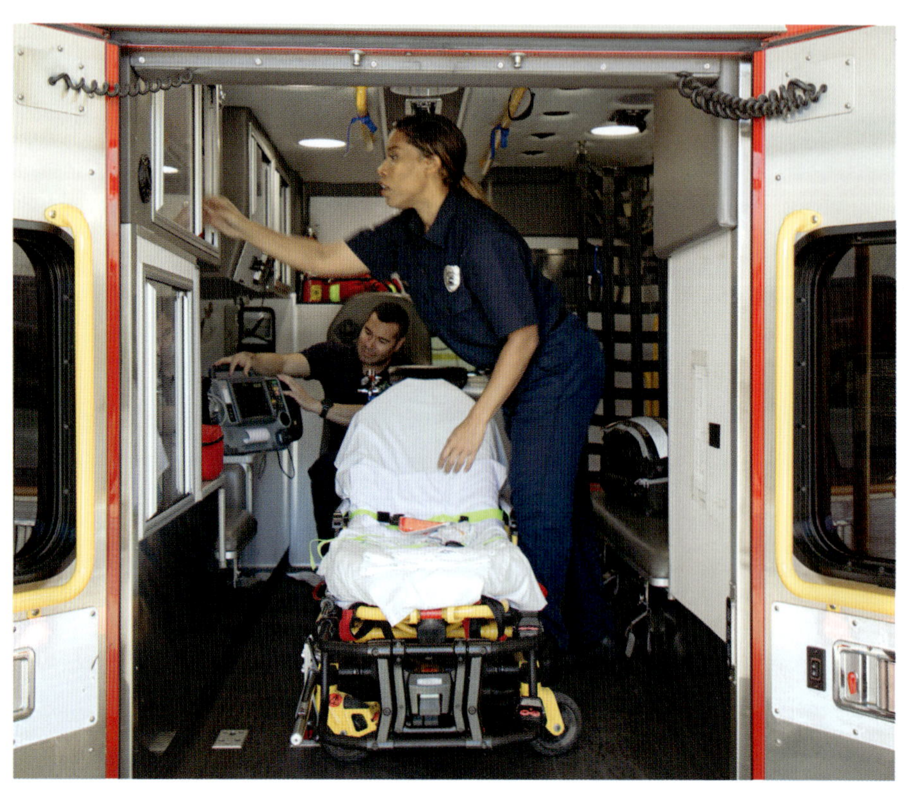

Working for emergency services may sound exciting, but it can be really scary, too. It's also hard work!

You can help emergency services by talking to parents and teachers about how to stay safe and avoid emergencies.

Remember: Don't call 9-1-1 unless there is an actual emergency. It will waste their time when they could be saving lives. Maybe one day you'll be the one saving lives!

Glossary

CPR
Cardiopulmonary resuscitation, a life-saving technique for a patient whose heart has stopped beating

Cyborg
A living thing enhanced by mechanical parts

Dispatcher
Someone who sends people where they are needed

Drill
Practice training

Emergency
Very serious and urgent situation

Evidence
Information gathered to prove that something is true

Fire extinguisher
A container that releases a jet of water, foam, gas, or other material to put out a fire

First aid
Immediate help for injury or illness

Germs
Tiny living things that can get into your body and make you sick

Hostages
People being held against their will

Illegal
Forbidden by law

Location
Particular position or place

Patrol
Keeping watch over an area

Siren
Alarm that makes a long, loud sound to warn people

Suspicious
Appearing to be doing something wrong

Technique
Way of doing something

Uniform
Clothing worn by members of the same group or organization

Volunteer
Someone who offers their time to work without being paid

Index

Quiz

Answer the questions to see what you have learned. Check your answers in the key below.

1. What number do you call for emergency services?
2. What can you do to help police stop crime?
3. True or False: Firefighting gear is very lightweight.
4. What does EMT stand for?
5. What sense do search-and-rescue dogs use to follow a trail?

1. 9-1-1 2. Report suspicious activity 3. False 4. Emergency medical technician 5. Their sense of smell